MEDITATION

FINDING THE SUPERSOUL WITHIN

Books by His Divine Grace
A.C. Bhaktivedanta Swami Prabhupāda:

Bhagavad-gītā As It Is
Śrīmad-Bhāgavatam (1st to 10th Cantos)
Śrī Caitanya-caritāmṛta (9 vols.)
Kṛṣṇa, The Supreme Personality of Godhead
Teachings of Lord Caitanya
The Nectar of Devotion
The Nectar of Instruction
Śrī Īśopaniṣad
Light of the Bhāgavata
Easy Journey to Other Planets
The Science of Self-Realization
Kṛṣṇa Consciousness: The Topmost Yoga System
Perfect Questions, Perfect Answers
Teachings of Lord Kapila, the Son of Devahuti
Transcendental Teachings of Prahlāda Mahārāja
Teachings of Queen Kuntī
Kṛṣṇa, the Reservoir of Pleasure
The Path of Perfection
Life Comes from Life
Message of Godhead
The Perfection of Yoga
Beyond Birth and Death
On the Way to Kṛṣṇa
Rāja-vidyā: The King of Knowledge
Elevation to Kṛṣṇa Consciousness
Kṛṣṇa Consciousness: The Matchless Gift
Selected Verses from the Vedic Scriptures
Back to Godhead magazine (founder)

A complete catalogue is available upon request.
The Bhaktivedanta Book Trust, ISKCON Temple, Hare Krishna Land, Juhu, Mumbai 400 049. India.
The above books are also available at ISKCON centers. Please contact a center near to your place.

MEDITATION

FINDING THE SUPERSOUL WITHIN

Assembled by

Drutakarmā Dāsa
Arcita Dāsa
Draviḍa Dāsa

The Bhaktivedanta Book Trust

Readers interested in the subject matter of this book are invited by The Bhaktivedanta Book Trust to correspond with its secretary at the following address:

The Bhaktivedanta Book Trust
ISKCON Temple,
Hare Krishna Land,
Juhu, Mumbai 400 049, India.

Website / E-mail :
www.indiabbt.com
admin@indiabbt.com

Meditation - Finding the Supersoul Within (English)

1st printing in India :25,000 copies
2nd to 3rd printing, December 2016: 1,05,000 copies
4th printing, December 2019: 70,000 copies

ISBN : 978-93-84564-88-9

On the cover - Authentic meditation gently peels away the layers of stress, tension, fear, and confusion of daily life and enables us to regain our connection to the Super Soul. Once that connection is made, life is filled with joy, harmony, balance, and peace.

Published and Printed by
The Bhaktivedanta Book Trust

C8AB

Content

Introduction

How are you doing in your relationship with your mind? Do you sometimes find it racing from thought to thought? Do you find it hard to concentrate? Do you have too much to think about? For some, the solution to getting some mental relief is television or intoxication. But others are finding a better way — meditation.

The benefits that you get from being able to free your mind from its routine cares and worries are enormous. You will feel enlivened and refreshed. You will find that you are able to focus on the essentials of life and not get caught up in all kinds of distracting side issues. But it all depends on performing the right kind of meditation in the right way.

Meditation has become quite popular and when something becomes popular, some people rush in to satisfy the demand with cheap imitations, for which they sometimes demand a high price. Of course, these commercial imitations do not deliver the results that people want, so they then become disappointed.

But the authentic meditation techniques are not like that. They are not the property of some group of people that can claim them as their own and market them like toothpaste or soap. Authentic meditation techniques are part of humanity's heritage. They belong to you already and there is no need to pay something for something that already belongs to you.

In this book, you will get an introduction to a practice of meditation that has been around for thousands of years. Although you are perhaps paying a little for this book, that is only because paper and ink cost money in today's society. You could get the same information for free, by walking into any one of the centers of ISKCON Temples.

In this book, you will learn the philosophical foundations of authentic meditation. The first thing to understand is the difference between the body, the mind and the conscious self. It is the conscious self who meditates, by focusing the mind. The mind has a tendency to wander, to follow the dictates of the body. By meditation the mind can be brought under control and when the mind is under control, the body is also under control. Instead of being led around by the mind and body into all kinds of difficult and frustrating situations, the conscious self is able to direct the mind and body in such a way that one's life becomes enjoyable, in the highest sense of the word. It's a great feeling, like being able to expertly play a musical instrument or expertly play a sport.

It is also important to understand that the conscious self has its source in a supreme conscious self, God. Somehow or other, most of us have lost our awareness of our connection with our source. And therefore we are not as happy as we could be. If we learn the authentic practice of meditation we can restore our living connection with our source and when that connection is there, knowledge, energy and pleasure flow to us to a greater degree than would otherwise be possible.

The most important meditation practice is *mantra* meditation. In this book, you will learn about the most effective *mantra* for the present times, the Hare Kṛṣṇa *mantra. Mantras* are made of names of God. Every great religion of the world recommends meditation on the names of God.

This book is based on the teachings of one of the greatest spiritual teachers of the modern age, His Divine Grace A.C. Bhaktivedanta Swami Prabhupāda (1896–1977). We have tried to distill the essence of these teachings, with the hope that after you have gone through this little book, you will look further into his works, which are a perfect guide to the purpose and practice of spiritual meditation, in all its forms.

Chapter One

Meditation: Its Practice and Goals

(by Drutakarmā Dāsa)

Millions of people, young and old, in countries all over the modern world are meditating. They are meditating in Paris and New York, in London and Lagos, in Sydney and Singapore, in Montreal and Moscow. More likely than not, one or more of your friends or relatives is a meditator. Why do these people meditate? Where and when did meditation originate?

The motive of many of those millions of meditators is simply to relieve stress. Meditation does in fact relieve stress, but its purpose goes far beyond that. The roots of meditation are to be found in the great religious traditions of the world, where the goal was understanding and realizing the ultimate truth about the self, the universe and God.

Judaism has a tradition of meditation that extends back through the Kabbalists of the Middle Ages to the time of the authors of the Psalms. In Christianity there have been several orders of contemplative monks and nuns and also several individual saints who have extolled the virtues of meditation. Islam has its own history of practitioners of meditation. And Buddhism has integrated the practice of meditation into its discipline. In one form or another, the practice of meditation may also be found among tribal peoples down through history, in all parts of the world. But the practice of meditation is most strongly associated with the Vedic tradition of ancient India.

Three Kinds of Spiritual Meditators

The goals of the various practitioners, in terms of their understanding of the self, God and universe, can be divided into three categories.

(1) Voidists. The voidists teach through meditation that we can understand that ultimately there is no soul, there is no God, there is no substantial universe. As long as we perceive the existence of self and God and universe, we suffer. The goal of these meditators is a state of nothingness, called nirvana, in which suffering ceases. Most Buddhist sects adhere to these voidist doctrines. The Buddhist goal of anatma, dissolution of the self and merging into the nothingness of nirvana, is an attempt to escape the difficulties we experience in the face of frustrated material desires. Although the oblivion of nothingness is attractive to some people, it is difficult to achieve. The underlying concept, that the self and the universe could have arisen from nothing, is illogical. A nothing that produces something is not nothing.

(2) Impersonalists. The impersonalists hold that through meditation we can understand that individual spiritual existence is an illusion, as is the existence of a substantial universe. But their ultimate goal is not

nothingness, as in the case of the voidists. For the impersonalists, God exists, but not as a person. God exists as an impersonal effulgence, a white light. In the state of enlightenment the individual self merges into the existence of this impersonal effulgence and thus becomes God. This view is propounded by the impersonal school of Vedic thought and can also be found in other spiritual traditions. Impersonalism, like the desire for nirvana, is a reaction to the frustration of unfulfilled material desires. But instead of merging into nothingness one desires to merge into an impersonal Absolute, destroying the distinction between soul and God. All is One. This position also has an illogical aspect. If we are all God, how did we get into the mess in which we now find ourselves? Obviously we are not identical to God. Also, if ultimately, everything is One, then where did the ignorance that covers the self's identity of God come from? That ignorance is a second thing, apart from God and therefore all is not One.

(3) Personalists. The personalists see the self as the eternal lover of an eternally existing Supreme Being who possesses all attractive personal features and qualities. They see through their meditation that this world is not an illusion. It is a real, but temporary, reflection of an eternally existing variegated spiritual world. There is a kind of nirvana in personal meditation. The goal of the personalist meditator is to make all thoughts other than thoughts of God zero. And there is also a kind of oneness in the personalist meditation. The meditator

does not wish to become one with God in the sense of becoming God, but in the sense of becoming one in purpose with God. Personalist meditation systems can be found in Christianity, Judaism, Islam and some theistic Buddhist schools of thought. Personalism is especially found among the theistic followers of the Vedic tradition, including the modern Kṛṣṇa consciousness movement. Their meditation is part of a *yoga* system called *bhakti-yoga,* the *yoga* of devotion.

Yoga and Meditation

Yoga has become extremely popular among people in the Western world. According to surveys by *yoga* organizations, about 20 million Americans practice *yoga* and over 100 million Americans are interested in learning about *yoga.* The same is true of people in countries all over the world. *Yoga* has become a truly international practice. Many *yoga* practitioners are aware of the ancient connection of *yoga* and spiritual meditation. The original goal of the *yoga* practices was not simply to keep the body firm and trim. The goal was to quiet all the urges and impulses of the body so that the mind could be steady. When the mind is steady, one can perceive one's identity beyond the body.

The most famous book of Indian spiritual philosophy is the *Bhagavad-gītā* (the Song of God). In that book, Lord Kṛṣṇa says (*Bg.* 6.18-19): "When the *yogī,* by practice of *yoga,* disciplines his mental activities and becomes situated in transcendence — devoid of all material desires — he is said to be well established in *yoga.* As a lamp in a windless place does not waver, so the transcendentalist, whose mind is controlled, remains always steady in his meditation on the transcendent self."

The transcendent self means the atma, the spirit soul, which illuminates the entire body with consciousness. But beyond this transcendent self one can also perceive another transcendent self, the Supersoul or Paramātmā. The Paramātmā is the localized presence of God in the hearts of all living things. The presence of the Lord in the Heart becomes visible to the perfected *yogī.* The Supersoul is an expansion of the one Supreme God, who is known by the Sanskrit name Kṛṣṇa, the All-Attractive.

In the *Gītā* (6.31), Kṛṣṇa says, "Such a *yogī,* who engages in the worshipful service of the Supersoul, knowing that I and the Supersoul are one, remains always in Me in all circumstances." That the purpose of *yoga* is to meditate on Kṛṣṇa is confirmed in the *Nārada-pañcarātra:* "By concentrating one's attention on the transcendental form of Kṛṣṇa, who is all-pervading and beyond time and space, one becomes absorbed in thinking of Kṛṣṇa and then attains the happy state of transcendental association with Him." This state of total concentration is called *samādhi.*

The Right System of Meditation for Today

In different ages, different methods of self realization are recommended. The physical *yoga* meditation system (*hatha yoga*) was recommended in very ancient times, when the environment and psychophysical characteristics of humans were more suited for it. *Hatha yoga* meditation was not meant for just an hour or so a day. It was meant to be one's total activity. The *hatha yogī* left home and went to the forest to practice *yoga* all day, every day. Today it is very difficult for a person to go to the forest and sit in a *yoga* posture for days and days. This is not to say that there is no benefit from doing some of the *hatha yoga* exercises, but by themselves they will not bring one to complete self and God realization.

There is, however, another *yoga* system that is better suited for people today and that is the *bhakti yoga* system. In *bhakti yoga,* the stilling of the senses by sitting in a physical hatha *yoga* posture is replaced by engaging the senses in the active service of the Supreme Soul. In this active *yoga,* the senses flow in harmony with the supreme. There is some partial reflection of this state in sports. Athletes sometimes speak of being "in the zone". When one is in the zone, one feels as if one were simply witnessing one's own activities. One no longer feels oneself to be the cause and one is not thinking of the results or rewards either. One simply become absorbed in the flow of the activity, for its own sake. This is, however, a temporary material state of mind. But if one practices active spiritual meditation properly, then one can be always in the flow of spiritual activity. And in that state one's consciousness becomes clear and quiet, like a still pond, even though one's bodily senses might be engaged in strenuous activity. Arjuna, the hero of the

Bhagavad-gītā, was a warrior. So his *yoga* was to fight. In the *Gītā* (8.7), Lord Kṛṣṇa told Arjuna: "You should always think of Me in the form of Kṛṣṇa and at the same time continue your prescribed duty of fighting. With your activities dedicated to Me and your mind and intelligence fixed on Me, you will attain Me without doubt." So the key to active meditational *yoga* is to act for the Supreme while meditating on the Supreme, just as we may think of a loved one while working.

Meditation on Transcendental Sound

There are several ways to meditate on Kṛṣṇa, but the most powerful method is *mantra* meditation. A *mantra* is a transcendental sound vibration composed of names of God. All the great religions of the world advise their followers to meditate on the name of God. The name of God is not different from God. It contains all the spiritual energies of God. According to Vedic philosophy, the energy of God is called *shakti.* This *shakti* exists in three main forms. *Sandhinī shakti* is the energy of existence. The energy of existence can situate us in a state beyond birth and death. In this state there is no longer any fear of non existence or death or disease. Then there is the *saṁvit shakti,* the energy of knowledge. When we are in contact with this energy, we know all that we need to know. We feel no lack of knowledge, we feel no influence of ignorance. Whatever we need to know is automatically revealed to us. Then finally there is the *hlādinī shakti,* the energy of pleasure. Kṛṣṇa, God, is the reservoir of all pleasure and we are also by nature meant to experience ever increasing spiritual pleasure. Contact with the *hlādinī shakti* allows us to do this. By meditating on the proper *mantras,* we get the benefits of the *sandhinī, saṁvit* and *hlādinī shakti.* We experience God and we experience our own selves as *sac-cid-ānanda-vigraha,* a form full of eternality, knowledge and pleasure, of the same substance as God. But although we experience ourselves as being of the same substance of God, we remain different in quantity. God is like the fire of spiritual potency and we are like sparks of that same potency. In the present times, the recommended *mantra* is the Hare Kṛṣṇa *mantra* : Hare Kṛṣṇa, Hare Kṛṣṇa, Kṛṣṇa Kṛṣṇa, Hare Hare, Hare Rāma, Hare Rāma, Rāma Rāma, Hare Hare. Hare, Rāma and Kṛṣṇa are names of God. Hare refers to the pleasure energy of God. Rāma refers to the spiritual strength of God. And Kṛṣṇa is a name of God that means all attractive. Other names of God exist in other languages and these names may also be meditated upon, according to one's preference.

Waking Up to New Realities Through Meditation

Meditation on the transcendental sound vibration of *mantras,* such as the Hare Kṛṣṇa *mantra,* can wake us up to new levels of reality. According to the Vedic teachings, our original nature is as spiritual beings, in the company of God, on the spiritual level of reality. If we depart from that original condition, we are placed into an artificial world of material sense impressions, amounting to a virtual reality system. We get some sense of this when we go to a movie theater. We go from the world of our real life into a dark room, where some images are projected onto a screen. If the film director and actors have done a good job, we give up our identification with our real selves and identify with the characters on the screen. We enter into this cinematic virtual reality system. So the world of our ordinary experience is something like that. We have forgotten our real selves and we have identified with a false self that is projected on the screen of our consciousness. It is as if we were sleeping and dreaming. But to remind us of our real condition, God injects real spiritual sense objects into our virtual reality. If we meditate upon these spiritual sense objects, then our consciousness is transformed. We wake up to our original self concept and our original concept of reality.

An alarm clock works in the same way. Imagine you are sleeping and are deeply involved in a dream. Outside the dream the alarm clock begins to beep. The sound of the beeping enters into our dream state. In the dream, we may hear the sound of the beeping as if it were part of the dream itself. Perhaps in the dream we are driving in a car and we hear the beeping of the clock as if it were the sound of another car's horn beeping. But if the mind continues to focus on the beeping sound, then our consciousness is transformed. Gradually or even quite suddenly, we wake up. We recognize the beeping sound as the beeping of our alarm clock. The dream disappears, along with our dream identity. We find ourselves in our bedroom, ready to get up and start another day in our waking reality.

Love of God, The Highest Ecstasy

When we enter the awakened state of spiritual reality, we find ourselves in the presence of God. But it is not a relationship of passive adoration. In the world of material experience, we find that we meditate more on persons and relationships rather than on lifeless things. In the path of spiritual meditation, the meditation upon our relationship with God becomes quite deep. It is often said that God is love, but this love is not some impersonal vague feeling. It is a deeply personal and individual reciprocal relationship that exists between each soul and God. Each soul has its unique loving relationship, but the relationship exists in five basic varieties, called *rasas* or flavors. One is the flavor of passive adoration. Another is servitorship. Another is friendship. Another is the parental relationship. And yet another is conjugal relationship, in which there is an exchange of spiritual emotions between the lover and beloved.

There are limitations to words, which can only serve to give us some hint of what lies ahead for those who practice the kind of transcendental meditation that will lead one into deeper and deeper states of realization of one's unique personal relationship with God, who is the reservoir of all loving relationships. And because every soul is part of God, when we establish our loving relationship with God, we also become fixed in loving relationships with all others with whom we come into contact.

Being in the Spiritual and Material Worlds Simultaneously

Amazingly, through the process of transcendental spiritual meditation, one can enter into these higher states of awareness even during the present life. One's experience of these higher states does not have to wait until death. One can be in this world, but not of it. Technically, this state is called *jivan mukta,* being liberated while still living in this world. In this state, one's external body and external affairs go on somewhat automatically, without much attention and effort on our part, while internally, we enter into deeper and deeper meditation upon God. We begin to see everything in connection with God.

The Final Goal

Nevertheless, the most important meditation we do takes place at the moment that the soul leaves the present body. In *Bhagavad-gītā* (8.6), Lord Kṛṣṇa says that whatever state of mind we enter at the time of death determines our destination in the next life. If our mental state is tinged with any of the modes of material nature, this will launch us into another body in the material world. There are three modes of material nature — goodness, passion and ignorance. If our mental state is tinged with the material mode of goodness, we will go to the higher material planets, the realms of the demigods and demigoddesses. These are the heavens and paradises found in some religions, where it is possible to enjoy material pleasures for vast periods of time. But this is still selfish and is still temporary. After the time of material enjoyment, one will fall again to the earthly level of reality, for another term of material existence. If our mental state is tinged with the material mode of passion, we remain on the earthly level of reality, in a human form. And if our mental state is tinged by the material mode of ignorance, then we enter into lower forms of life or into lower planets. But if our mental state is fully transcendental, if we are one hundred percent focused on God, then we will achieve a different destination. The *Śrīmad-Bhāgavatam* (1.9.23) states: "The Personality of Godhead, who appears in the mind of the devotee by attentive devotion and meditation and by chanting of the holy name, releases the devotee from the bondage of fruitive activities at the time of his quitting the material body." Instead of entering a material body in the material world, the soul will enter into the spiritual world. This is the actual goal of any genuine system of meditation.

Chapter 2

Practical Meditation for the Modern Age

In this lecture Śrīla Prabhupāda explains the process of meditation taught by Lord Kṛṣṇa in the *Bhagavad-gītā.* Śrīla Prabhupāda points out that although the details of the process Kṛṣṇa outlines here are impractical for nearly everyone in the modern age, the essence of the process—absorption of the mind in thought of the Supreme—is easily available through the practice of *bhakti-yoga.*

śucau deśe pratiṣṭhāpya
sthiram āsanam ātmanaḥ
nāty-ucchritaṁ nāti-nīcaṁ
cailājina-kuśottaram

tatraikāgraṁ manaḥ kṛtvā
yata-cittendriya-kriyaḥ
upaviśyāsane yuñjyād
yogam ātma-viśuddhaye

"To practice *yoga,* one should go to a secluded, sacred place, lay kuśa grass on the ground and then cover the grass with a deerskin and a soft cloth. The seat should be neither too high nor too low. The *yogī* should then sit on the seat very firmly and practice *yoga* by controlling the mind and the senses, purifying the heart and fixing the mind on one point." [*Bhagavad-gītā* 6.11-12]

These are Kṛṣṇa's practical instructions on how to execute mystic *yoga.* In the United States *yoga* is very popular and there are many so-called *yoga* societies that follow various teachings. But here the Supreme Lord Himself is giving instructions on how to practice *yoga.* The first instruction concerns how to sit and where to sit. First one has to select a place where he can sit down and practice *yoga.* Kṛṣṇa says it should be in a "sacred place", which refers to a place of pilgrimage. In India the transcendentalists (the *yogīs* and devotees) all leave home and reside in sacred places-such as Prayag, Mathurā, Vṛndāvana, Hṛṣīkeśa or Hardwar and they practice *yoga* there. But in this age how many people are prepared to search out a sacred place? For their livelihood they have to live in a congested city. What is the question of finding a sacred place? But if one can't find a sacred place, then how can he practice *yoga,* since that is the first instruction?

The answer is found in *bhakti-yoga.* In the *bhakti-yoga* system the sacred place is the Lord's temple. A temple is *nirguṇa* or transcendental. The Vedic injunction is that the city is the place of passion, the forest is the place of goodness and the Lord's temple is transcendental. If one lives in a city or a town, he is living in a passionate place. And if he doesn't want to live in a passionate place, he can go to a forest-that is a place of goodness. But God's temple is above passion and goodness. Therefore a temple is the only secluded place in this age. We cannot go to a secluded place in a forest; it is impossible. And if one makes a show of *yoga* practice in a so-called class and indulges in all kinds of nonsensical things, that is not real *yoga.* Here are the genuine instructions on how to practice *yoga.*

Concerning the actual process of meditation, the *Bṛhan-nāradīya Purāṇa* says that in the Kali-yuga (the present yuga or age), when people in general are short-lived, slow in spiritual realization and always disturbed by various anxieties, the best means of spiritual realization is to chant the holy name of the Lord:

harer nāma harer nāma
harer nāma eva kevalam
kalau nāsty eva nāsty eva
nāsty eva gatir anyathā

"In this age of quarrel and hypocrisy, the only means of deliverance is chanting the holy name of the Lord. There is no other way. There is no other way. There is no other way." This chanting of Hare Kṛṣṇa, which is the essence of the *bhakti-yoga* process, is universal and it is so nice that even a child can take part in it. But other processes will not be feasible.

Two of these processes are *aṣṭāṅga-yoga* and *jñāna-yoga.* The sitting postures and meditation comprise *aṣṭāṅga-yoga* and *jñāna-yoga* is an analytical and philosophical process by which one tries to understand what is Brahman and what is not Brahman (neti neti). Part of *jñāna-yoga* consists of studying the *Vedānta-sūtra,* which begins with these words: *Janmādy asya yataḥ.* This aphorism gives us the hint that the Supreme Brahman, the Absolute Truth, is that from which everything has emanated. Then we must try to understand what that Absolute Truth is. The nature of the Absolute Truth is explained in the first verse of *Śrīmad-Bhāgavatam: janmādy asya yato 'anvayād itarataś ca artheṣu abhijñaḥ svarāṭ.*

Now, if the Absolute Truth is the supreme cause of all emanations, then what are His symptoms? The *Bhāgavatam* says that He must be cognizant. He's not dead. And what kind of cognizance does He have? *Anvayād itarataś cārtheṣu:* "He is directly and indirectly cognizant of all manifestations." I am cognizant, as is every living being, but I do not know how many hairs there are on my body. And if I ask anyone else, "Do you know how many hairs you have on your body?" he will not be able to answer. Another example of cognizance: I know I am eating, but I do not know how my internal processes are working — how the food is being transformed, how it is entering my bloodstream, how the blood is going through the arteries and veins. I do not know any of this. So, this kind of knowledge is not real knowledge.

But the Supreme, says the *Bhāgavatam,* knows everything, directly and indirectly. God must know everything — He must know what is going on in every corner of His creation. In other words, the Supreme

Truth, from whom everything has emanated, must be supremely cognizant (*abhijñaḥ*). Now, one may say, "If God is so powerful, wise and cognizant, then He must have learned His knowledge from someone similar." No. If a person has learned His knowledge from someone else, then he is not God. God is *svarāṭ* or independent. He knows everything automatically.

So, this is *jñāna-yoga:* to investigate by philosophical inquiry the nature of the Supreme, from whom everything is emanating. And because the Supreme is explained in *Śrīmad-Bhāgavatam,* the *Bhāgavatam* teaches the supreme *jñāna-yoga* and *bhakti-yoga* combined. In *bhakti-yoga* the target is the same as in the other *yogas.* The *jñāna-yoga* tries to reach the supreme, ultimate, goal by philosophical analysis, the *aṣṭāṅga-yogī* tries to concentrate his mind on the Supreme and the *bhakti-yogī* simply engages himself in serving the Supreme Lord so that He reveals Himself. The *jñānīs* and mystic *yogīs* try to understand the Lord by the ascending process of knowledge and the *bhaktas* understand Him by the descending process.

For example, if we are in the darkness of night and we try to understand what the sun is by the ascending process, by shining our very powerful searchlight, we cannot see the sun. But if we use the descending process, then when the sun rises we understand it immediately. The ascending process is the process of induction — using our own endeavor to gain knowledge and the descending process is deduction. Another example: Suppose I am trying to know whether man is mortal. If I go to my father and he says that man is mortal and if I accept it, then I have understood the truth by the deductive process. But if I want to use the inductive process to learn whether man is mortal, then I have to study many thousands of men and see whether they are immortal or mortal. This will take so much time and my knowledge will never be complete. But if I take the knowledge that man is mortal from a superior authority, then my knowledge is complete. Thus, in *Śrīmad-Bhāgavatam* [10.14.29] it is said,

athāpi te deva padāmbuja-dvaya-
prasāda-leśānugṛhīta eva hi
jānāti tattvaṁ bhagavan-mahimno
na cānya eko 'pi ciraṁ vicinvan

"My dear Lord, a person who has received a little favor from You can understand You very quickly. But those who are trying to understand You by the ascending process may go on speculating for millions of years, yet they will never understand You."

The speculators come to the point of frustration and confusion. "God is zero", they say. If God is zero, then how have so many forms come into being? God is not zero. The *Vedānta-sūtra* says, *janmādy asya yataḥ:* "Everything is generated from the Supreme." Now, we have to study how it is generated. That is also explained in the *Vedānta-sūtra. Veda* means "knowledge" and *anta* means "ultimate". So *Vedānta* means "the ultimate knowledge". The ultimate knowledge is realization of the Supreme Lord.

Devotee: Śrīla Prabhupāda, you said that we cannot comprehend the form of Kṛṣṇa with our mind and senses. Then how are we to understand the form of Kṛṣṇa that we see in the pictures and the *mūrtis* [statues]?

Śrīla Prabhupāda: You should simply serve Him; then He will reveal Himself. You cannot understand Kṛṣṇa by the ascending process. You have to serve Kṛṣṇa and Kṛṣṇa will reveal Himself to you. This is stated in *Bhagavad-gītā* [10.11]:

teṣām evānukampārtham
aham ajñāna-jaṁ tamaḥ
nāśayāmy ātma-bhāva-stho
jñāna-dīpena bhāsvatā

"Just as a special favor to those who always engage in My service, I vanquish all kinds of darkness and ignorance with the light of knowledge." Kṛṣṇa is within you and when you are sincerely searching after Kṛṣṇa by the devotional process, He reveals Himself to you. As Kṛṣṇa says in the Eighteenth Chapter of *Bhagavad-gītā, bhaktyā mām abhijānāti:* "One can understand Me only by *bhakti,* the devotional process." And what is *bhakti? Bhakti* is this: *śravaṇaṁ kīrtanaṁ viṣṇoḥ,* simply hearing and chanting about Viṣṇu. This is the beginning of *bhakti.* So, if you simply hear talks on Kṛṣṇa sincerely and submissively, then you will understand Kṛṣṇa. Kṛṣṇa will reveal Himself to you. Now we are hearing about Kṛṣṇa from *Bhagavad-gītā* and chanting His glories: Hare Kṛṣṇa, Hare Kṛṣṇa, Kṛṣṇa Kṛṣṇa, Hare Hare/Hare

Rāma, Hare Rāma, Rāma Rāma, Hare Hare. This is the beginning — *śravaṇaṁ kīrtanaṁ viṣṇoḥ.* Everything is done in relation to Viṣṇu. The meditation is on Viṣṇu, the *bhakti* is for Viṣṇu — nothing is without Viṣṇu. And Kṛṣṇa is the original form of Viṣṇu (*Kṛṣṇa tu bhagavān svayam*), the original form of the Supreme Personality of Godhead. So, if we follow this process of *bhakti-yoga,* then we'll be able to understand the form of Kṛṣṇa, without any doubt.

The next verses of *Bhagavad-gītā* read as follows:

samaṁ kāya-śiro-grīvaṁ
dhārayann acalaṁ sthiraḥ
samprekṣya nāsikāgraṁ svaṁ
diśaś cānavalokayan

praśāntātmā vigata-bhīr
brahmacāri-vrate sthitaḥ
manaḥ saṁyamya mac-citto
yukta āsīta mat-paraḥ

"One should hold one's body, neck and head in a straight line and stare steadily at the tip of the nose. Thus, with an unagitated, subdued mind, devoid of fear, completely free from sex life, one should meditate upon Me within the heart and make Me the ultimate goal of life." [*Bg.* 6.13-14]

The goal of life is to know Kṛṣṇa, who is situated within the heart of every living being as Paramātmā, the four-handed Viṣṇu form. The *aṣṭāṅga-yoga* process is practiced in order to discover and see this localized form of Viṣṇu and not for any other purpose. One who has no program to realize this Viṣṇu-murti is uselessly engaged in *mock-yoga* practice and is certainly wasting his time. Kṛṣṇa is the ultimate goal of life and the Viṣṇu-murti situated in one's heart is the object of *aṣṭāṅga-yoga* practice. As mentioned in the previous verses, to begin the *aṣṭāṅga-yoga* process one must first of all select a solitary place, where he can execute *yoga* alone. It is not that one can go to a *yoga* class, pay some fee, do some gymnastics and then come back home and do all kinds of nonsense. We shouldn't be entrapped by all these ridiculous "*yoga* societies". Such societies, I can declare, are simply societies of the cheaters and the cheated. Here in *Bhagavad-gītā* is the real *yoga* process, taught by the supreme authority, Kṛṣṇa. Can there possibly be any person who is a better *yogī* than Kṛṣṇa? No. And here is His authoritative statement on *yoga.* So, first of all one has to select a secluded, holy place and prepare a special seat. Then one has to sit down upon the seat in an erect posture: "One should hold one's body, neck and head in a straight line." These things help to concentrate the mind, that's all. But the real purpose of *yoga* is to keep Kṛṣṇa always within oneself. Here it is stated, "One should hold one's body, neck and head in a straight line and stare steadily at the tip of the nose." And if one closes his eyes during meditation, he'll sleep. I have seen this. In these "*yoga* classes" so many so-called meditators are simply sleeping, because as soon as one closes his eyes, it is natural that he'll feel sleepy. So the eyes must be half-closed and one has to see the tip of his nose. This process will help the mind to be fixed.

Then Kṛṣṇa says one should have an "unagitated, subdued mind, devoid of fear". Generally, a *yogī* practices in a jungle. But if he's thinking, "Is some tiger or snake coming? What is that?" his mind will be agitated. After all, he has to sit down alone in a jungle. There are so many animals — tigers, lions, snakes. Therefore it is especially stated here that the *yogī* must be "devoid of fear". The skin of a deer is especially used in *yoga-āsana* because it has some chemical property that repels snakes. If one sits down on that particular skin, the snakes and other reptiles will not come. That is the purpose of the deerskin: one will not be disturbed. But one can be truly fearless only when one is fully in Kṛṣṇa consciousness. A conditioned soul is fearful due to his perverted memory, his forgetfulness of his eternal relationship with Kṛṣṇa. *Śrīmad-Bhāgavatam* says, *bhayaṁ dvitīyābhiniveśataḥ syād īśād apetasya viparyayo 'smṛtiḥ.* Kṛṣṇa consciousness is the only basis for fearlessness. Therefore perfect *yoga* practice is possible only for a person who is Kṛṣṇa conscious. The next qualification for the *yogī* is that he must be "completely free from sex life". If one indulges in sex, he cannot fix his mind on anything. A steady mind is the effect of brahmacarya or celibacy. If one remains a brahmacārī or without sex life, then he can be determined. A practical example is Mahatma Gandhi, of India. Now, he started his movement of non-violent non-cooperation against the powerful British Empire. Just see! He declared, "I shall fight with the Britishers nonviolently, without any weapon." Besides, India was dependent, so there were no weapons. And the few times armed revolutions were attempted, the Britishers, being more powerful, cut them down. So Gandhi invented the method of non-violent non-cooperation. "I shall fight with the Britishers", he declared, "and even if they become violent, I shall not become violent. In this way I shall get world sympathy." This was his plan. He was a great statesman, but more important, his determination was very fixed because he was a brahmacārī. At the age of thirty-six he gave up sex life. He was a young family man — he had children, he had a wife — but from the age of thirty-six on he gave up sex with his wife. That made him so determined to drive away the Britishers from the land of India that he actually did it. Therefore, refraining from sex makes one very powerful. Even if one doesn't do anything else, if he simply refrains from sex he becomes a very powerful man. People do not know the secret: if one wants to do anything with determination, one has to stop sex.

Therefore in no Vedic process — neither the *yoga* process nor the *bhakti* process nor the *jñāna* process — is unrestricted sex indulgence allowed. No. Sex indulgence is allowed only in family life, just to beget very nice children, that's all. Sex is not for sense enjoyment, although there is enjoyment by nature's arrangement. Unless there were enjoyment, why would anyone take responsibility for family life? That pleasure is nature's gift, but we should not take advantage of it. These are the secrets of life.

So *yoga* practice is such a nice thing, but if one simultaneously indulges in sex life, it is simply nonsense. It is simply nonsense if anyone says that one can go on with his sex life as much as he likes and at the same time become a *yogī.* The so-called *yoga* teachers advertise, "Simply pay my fees and I will give you a miracle *mantra.*" These things are all nonsense. But we accept them because we want to be cheated. We want to get something sublime very cheaply. That means we want to be cheated. If I want a very fine thing, I must pay for it. Suppose I go to a store and say to the proprietor, "Sir, I can pay you ten cents. Please give me the best thing in your store." How can I expect the best thing for ten cents? If I want to purchase gold, then I have to pay for it. Similarly, if we want perfection in *yoga* practice, then we have to pay for it by giving up sex. That is the instruction of *Bhagavad-gītā.* We shouldn't try to make *yoga* a childish affair. If we try to make it a childish affair, then we'll be cheated. And there are so many cheaters waiting to cheat us, take our money and go away. Here is the authoritative statement: "Free from sex life".

Next Kṛṣṇa says, "One should meditate upon Me". Ultimately, what is the object of meditation? Not the void, but the form of Viṣṇu. This is *sāṅkhya-yoga,* which was first practiced by Kapiladeva, an incarnation of Kṛṣṇa or God. So the secret of *yoga* is that one should absorb the mind in Kṛṣṇa. The process of sitting straight and seeing the tip of one's nose helps one to concentrate the mind on the Viṣṇu form or Kṛṣṇa. "One should meditate upon Me", says Kṛṣṇa. Thus meditation in *sāṅkhya-yoga* means meditation on Kṛṣṇa.

Now, in the Kṛṣṇa consciousness movement the meditation is directly on Kṛṣṇa and nothing else. Therefore no one is a better meditator than my disciples. They are concentrating simply on Kṛṣṇa and all their activities are centered on Kṛṣṇa. When they're working in the garden, digging the earth, they're thinking, "A nice rose will grow and we shall offer it to Kṛṣṇa." This is meditation — practical meditation: "I shall grow a rose and it will be offered to Kṛṣṇa." Even in the digging there is meditation. And when they are preparing nice food, they think, "It will be eaten by Kṛṣṇa." So, in cooking there is meditation. And what to speak of chanting Hare Kṛṣṇa and dancing.

Therefore, because they are meditating twenty-four hours a day on Kṛṣṇa, my disciples are perfect *yogīs.* Let anyone come and challenge them. We are teaching the perfect *yoga* system, but not whimsically: on the authority of the *Bhagavad-gītā.* We have not manufactured anything by concoction. Here is Kṛṣṇa's statement that one should simply concentrate one's mind on Him and my disciples' activities have been so molded that they cannot think of anything but Kṛṣṇa. So they are the highest meditators. Kṛṣṇa says, "Think of Me within the heart and make Me the ultimate goal of life."

Kṛṣṇa is the ultimate goal of life and my disciples are preparing themselves for being transferred to Kṛṣṇa's planet (Kṛṣṇaloka). Kṛṣṇa consciousness, therefore, is the perfect *yoga*.

Chapter Three

Three Histories of Successful Meditators

For thousands of years, the greatest spiritual teachers of India have used historical narrations found in *Śrīmad-Bhāgavatam,* such as the one that follows, to illustrate for their disciples the principles of meditation. *Śrīmad-Bhāgavatam,* an epic philosophical and literary classic, holds a prominent position in India's voluminous written wisdom. The timeless knowledge of India is expressed in the *Vedas,* ancient Sanskrit texts that touch upon all fields of human understanding. Known as "the ripened fruit of the tree of Vedic literature," *Śrīmad-Bhāgavatam* is the most complete and authoritative exposition of Vedic knowledge.

The scientific principles of meditation do not change with the passage of time; they remain constant and these timeless stories are as relevant to the modern seeker as they were to those who sought enlightenment in bygone ages.

Millions of years ago, the world was ruled by a king named Uttanapada. He had two wives, Suruci and *Sunīti.* Though *Sunīti* was the mother of his eldest son, the five-year-old Dhruva, Suruci was his favorite.

One day Dhruva saw his father fondling his half-brother Uttama on his lap and wanted to join him. But Suruci called out harshly: “Stop, Dhruva! You can’t join my son Uttama on your father’s throne until you perform severe austerities for many years, satisfy Lord Vāsudeva, God Himself and then take birth again from me in your next life!”

Stung by Suruci’s words, Dhruva began to breathe heavily in anger. He looked to his father for support, but the king avoided his glance and remained silent. Dhruva ran out of the palace and headed for his mother’s modest house nearby. When he reached Sunīti’s place, his lips were still trembling and he was crying, so some palace residents told Sunīti what had happened. Hearing about the insult to her son, she joined him in his grief.

Though burning within, Sunīti composed herself and spoke to Dhruva through her tears:

“My dear son, please do not bear any ill will toward your stepmother. One who hurts others suffers from that pain himself. The king favors her and neglects me and there’s nothing you or I can do about that”.

“But her instruction, though hard to hear, is good for you. If you want to sit on the throne one day, then you should at once begin worshiping the lotus feet of Lord Vāsudeva, the Supreme Personality of Godhead. Your great-grandfather Brahma did this and was blessed with the power to create this whole universe and your grandfather Svāyambhuva Manu did the same and received all material happiness and at the end, liberation from birth and death and all suffering. So take shelter of the Lord without delay. Meditate deeply on Him within your heart and at every moment serve Him with devotion. Surely He alone can relieve your distress and bestow the blessings you desire."

Taking his mother's instructions to heart, Dhruva — whose very name means "fixed" — left his father's palace with great determination in search of God.

The great sage Nārada heard about Dhruva's leaving the palace and was struck with wonder. The sage approached the boy, touched him gently on the head as a blessing and spoke as follows:

"How wonderful is the warrior caste! The fighters cannot stand even a slight insult. Just imagine! Though only a small boy, this Dhruva could not bear the harsh words of his stepmother."

Then Nārada decided to test Dhruva's determination to see if he was fit to undergo the rigors of meditative *yoga.* Thus the sage addressed the boy:

"My dear child, give up your grief at your stepmother's insult. Your sorrow is simply the work of the Lord's illusory energy. Everyone must suffer or enjoy according to his previous activities. This is the law of karma. A wise man sees the Lord's hand in everything and is satisfied with whatever befalls him, good or bad".

"Now, following your mother's advice, you have decided to undertake the process of mystic meditation to win the Lord's favor. But you're just a small boy! Even grown men find the austerities involved in this process impossible to bear. In fact, there are many highly qualified mystic *yogīs* who practiced this process for many births, spending countless days in deep meditative trance, but still failed to find the end of the path of God realization".

"So go home, Dhruva. If you persist now, you'll fail. When you are mature, by the Lord's grace you can execute this mystic *yoga* meditation. Till then, be equipoised in happiness and distress. When you meet a superior, be joyful, when you meet an inferior, show compassion and when you meet an equal, make friends with him. This is your path to enlightenment now."

Dhruva replied, "My dear sage, thank you for your instructions on how to become equipoised in this world of pain and pleasure. But my warrior's pride will not let me accept them, for my stepmother's cruel words have cut me to the quick. O wise soul, magnanimous like the sun, I long for a position more exalted than anyone has achieved till now, even my father, grandfather and great-grandfather. If you can help me, please teach me a righteous path to that goal."

Nārada, feeling moved by Dhruva's appeal, then addressed the lad with deep compassion:

"My dear child, in truth your mother Sunīti's instructions are perfect for you. Simply meditate deeply on the Supreme Lord, Vāsudeva and serve Him with devotion. Indeed, this path is auspicious for all. Here's how to go about it.

"First go to the bank of the Yamunā River in Vṛndāvana. There search out the holy forest of

Madhuvana and begin bathing in the Yamunā's waters morning, noon and evening. After each bath, sit for *yoga* meditation, employing the breathing process known as *prāṇāyāma* to control your mind and senses. Then with great patience begin meditating on the Lord's form within your heart."

"The Lord's face, with eyes and lips reddish like the rising sun, is very beautiful and pleasing, expressing His love for His devotees. His form is always youthful, its every limb perfect. An ocean of mercy, He is always eager to protect His surrendered devotees. His complexion is deep bluish, a fresh garland graces His chest and He bears a conch shell, discus, club and lotus flower in His four hands."

"He wears silken yellow garments, a pearl necklace and a priceless bejeweled helmet, along with gem-studded bracelets and armlets. Golden ankle bells and waist bells tinkle as He walks. He is always peaceful and very pleasing to the eyes and mind."

"Real *yogīs* meditate on this transcendental form of the Lord as He stands on the center of the lotus of their hearts, His gemlike toe nails glittering. Try to constantly see this smiling form of Vāsudeva in your heart and contemplate the all-auspicious transcendental activities He performs in His various incarnations. If you meditate in this way, you will very soon be freed of all material contamination."

"Most important, my dear Dhruva, you must chant the *mantra oṁ namo bhagavate vāsudevāya* with great concentration and devotion as you meditate on the Lord in your heart. You should also worship the Lord externally in the form of His sacred statue made of earth. If you meditate and worship in this way, thus seriously and sincerely rendering devotional service to the Lord, He will surely bless you according to your desire."

Taking the instructions of his *guru* Nārada to heart, Dhruva headed for Madhuvana. After arriving, he bathed in the Yamunā River and fasted through the night. The next morning he began his *yoga* meditation with all seriousness and determination.

The first month Dhruva ate only fruits and berries every third day—just enough to keep body and soul together—all the while meditating on the Lord within and chanting *oṁ namo bhagavate vāsudevāya.*

The second month Dhruva continued his meditation, eating only dry grass and leaves every sixth day.

The third month Dhruva drank water only every ninth day and achieved unbroken absorption in his meditation on the Lord.

The fourth month Dhruva attained total mastery of *prāṇāyāma,* breathing only every twelfth day as his absorption in thought of the Lord deepened.

By the fifth month, Dhruva had controlled his breathing so perfectly that he was able to rise up from his meditation seat and stand on only one leg, as immovable as a pillar. Completely controlling his senses, without the slightest distraction he fixed his mind on the *mantra* and the form of the Supreme Lord within.

When Dhruva had thus mentally captured the Lord, the refuge of the total material creation and master of all living beings, the universe began to tremble. The pressure of Dhruva's big toe displaced the earth in its orbit, just as an elephant on a boat might rock it from side to side with every step. Indeed, Dhruva had become practically as heavy as the Lord due to his total absorption in meditation on Him. Moreover, by Dhruva's closing all the holes in his body and restraining his breath, the total universal breathing was choked and all the demigods felt suffocated.

In desperation, the demigods prayed to Lord Vāsudeva: "Dear Lord, we and all other living beings are suffocating due to some unknown cause. Please save us!"

The Lord replied, "My dear demigods, do not fear. Your plight is due to the severe austerities of Dhruva, who is now fully absorbed in meditating on Me. I shall stop his meditation now and relieve your suffering."

Reassured, the demigods bowed to the Lord and returned to their heavenly planets.

Then Lord Vāsudeva mounted His bird-carrier Garuda and went to Madhuvana Forest to see His servant Dhruva.

As Dhruva meditated in deep trance on the form of the Lord within his heart, suddenly the Lord disappeared. The child became perturbed and his meditation broke. But when he opened his eyes he saw the same form of the Lord present before him. Dhruva became greatly agitated in his ecstasy and fell to the ground like a rod to offer the Lord his respects. Then as he arose, absorbed in love of God, he gazed upon the Lord as if he were drinking in the Lord's beauty with his eyes and embracing Him with his arms.

Dhruva wanted to offer beautiful Sanskrit prayers to the Lord, but he felt unable, being after all only a small boy. The Lord saw Dhruva's eagerness and touched His conch shell to Dhruva's forehead as the boy stood entranced before Him. That conch-shell touch infused Dhruva with perfect awareness of the deepest Vedic truths — indeed, Dhruva now completely understood the Personality of Godhead and His relationship with all living entities. Thus Dhruva offered his conclusive prayers:

"My dear all-powerful Lord, You have entered within my heart and enlivened all my sleeping senses, especially my power of speech. Let me offer my respectful obeisances unto You. My Lord, though You are one and indivisible, You expand Your potencies in both the spiritual and material worlds. Then You enter the material cosmos as the Supersoul and create untold varieties of manifestations through the modes of material nature."

"You are the only friend of all who want final liberation from all suffering, but I was so foolish that I prayed to You for the sense gratification of this bag of skin called the material body. I ardently wanted to occupy a post even greater than Lord Brahma's and to that end I undertook severe austerities and practiced an extremely difficult form of meditation. But now that I have achieved a direct vision of You — a vision rare even among the great demigods — I realize that compared to this divine jewel, my aspired-for kingdom is like broken glass. O Lord, I am fully satisfied with this vision and now want no other benediction from You."

"But if You want to bestow Your blessings on me, here is my request: Please bless me so that I may associate with Your great and pure devotees who constantly engage in Your transcendental loving service, as the waves of a river constantly flow. In their company I shall drink the intoxicating beverage of Your glories and thus easily cross the treacherous ocean of repeated birth and death."

Having heard Dhruva's prayers, the Lord replied: "My dear Dhruva, you have executed your difficult vow to perfection. All good fortune to you! I know that within your heart you maintained throughout your meditation a desire for a fabulous kingdom greater than Lord Brahmā's. So although your desire is very ambitious and difficult to fulfill, I shall fulfill it."

"My dear Dhruva, in your next life I shall award you the glowing planet known as the polestar, which will continue to exist even after the destruction of the universe. Indeed, this planet, known as Viṣṇupāda, is part of Vaikuṇṭha, My eternal abode."

"But before then, when your father retires you will sit on the throne and rule the world dharmically for thirty-six thousand years. During that time all your senses will remain as strong as they are now — you will never age. Thus you will be able to enjoy all happiness in this life while always remembering Me. This remembrance, the fruit of your meditation, will insure that you are transported to Vaikuṇṭha at the time of death."

After Dhruva had worshiped Lord Vāsudeva and the Lord had departed for His own abode, Dhruva felt torn between jubilation and regret. He was overjoyed that he would return to the spiritual world at the end of his life and rejoin the Lord, but he was sorry that he had prayed for a great kingdom during his meditation and thus been required to rule the world for thirty-six thousand years.

Still, when he came of age and his father retired, Dhruva performed his duty faithfully, acting as the perfect king and finally he himself retired from the throne and entrusted it to his eldest son. Leaving behind the great riches and comforts of his royal position, he traveled to Badarikāśrama in the Himalayas. After bathing in the crystal-clear water of a mountain stream, he sat in meditation and fixed the form of the Lord in his heart. Soon Dhruva entered into deep trance and became overwhelmed with love of God. His heart melted in transcendental ecstasy, tears flowed from his eyes and his bodily hairs stood on end.

Just then a beautiful effulgent airplane descended from the sky. Riding upon it were Nanda and Sunanda, two extremely handsome associates of the Lord. Dhruva showed them respect by standing up at once and then bowing with folded hands.

One of the Lord's associates said to Dhruva: "My dear king, all good fortune to you! Listen carefully. Your great austerities and meditation on Vāsudeva many years ago have qualified you to go to Viṣṇupāda, the Vaikuṇṭha planet in this universe. No one else has ever gone there from this material plane, but you are welcome. Please come and live with us there eternally."

Dhruva at once took a sacred bath, dressed and performed his daily spiritual rituals. Then he offered respects to the sages who had gathered for the joyous occasion and circumambulated the airplane out of respect. Dhruva began to glow with pure spiritual effulgence.

Just then death personified approached Dhruva. Ordinary persons are overwhelmed with fear as death approaches, but Dhruva simply stepped on the head of death and entered the Vaikuṇṭha airplane. Auspicious sounds of drumming and singing resounded from the heavens as flowers showered from above.

As the plane began its trip to Vaikuṇṭha, Dhruva had only one worry: What was to become of his mother, Sunīti? How could he go back to Godhead without her? Nanda and Sunanda then reassured Dhruva by pointing out another airplane following theirs and carrying his mother to the same destination. Thus Dhruva was at last at peace, knowing he had accomplished his life's mission.

Lessons from the history of Dhruva Mahārāja:

1. To achieve our goals in life we should worship the Supreme Personality of Godhead and no one else.

2. One should tolerate insults without being disturbed, for such disturbance is a feature of illusion. Śrīla Prabhupāda: "An intelligent person, therefore, should be always satisfied, depending on the mercy of the Lord."

3. One should begin devotional service at any stage of life, even childhood, for there is no precondition for practicing devotional service. Even if one is filled with material desires, one should begin devotional service. Śrīla Prabhupāda: "It is not a fact, however, that those who have material desires are prohibited from worshiping the Supreme Personality of Godhead. This is the essential instruction from the life of Dhruva."

4. The object for meditation should be the form and name of God and one should also worship that form externally as a *murti* or sacred statue.

5. One should be very determined to overcome all obstacles on the path of God realization and achieve success — liberation from material entanglement and return to the kingdom of God.

Our next narration comes from Śrī Caitanya-caritāmṛta, a book written in Sanskrit and Bengali in the 16th century by the exalted devotee-saint Śrīla Kṛṣṇadāsa Kavirāja. Here he describes an incident in the life of Haridāsa Ṭhākura, who is known among the followers of Lord Caitanya as namācārya, "the exemplar for chanting the holy name."

After leaving his home, Haridāsa Ṭhākura stayed for some time in the forest of Benāpola, a village in Bengal about a hundred miles north of present-day Kolkata. Haridāsa Ṭhākura constructed a cottage in a solitary forest. There he planted a sacred tulasī plant and in front of that plant he would chant the holy name of the Lord 300,000 times daily. He chanted throughout the entire day and night. For his bodily maintenance he would go to a *brāhmaṇa's* house and beg some food. He was spiritually so influential that all the neighboring people worshiped him.

A landholder named Rāmacandra Khān was the zamindar of that district. He was envious of the Lord's devotees and was therefore a great atheist. Unable to tolerate that such respect was being offered to Haridāsa Ṭhākura, Rāmacandra Khān planned in various ways to dishonor him. By no means could he find any fault in the character of Haridāsa Ṭhākura. Therefore he called for local prostitutes and hatched a plan to discredit Haridāsa.

Rāmacandra Khān said to the prostitutes, "There's a mendicant named Haridāsa residing nearby. All of you devise a way to deviate him from his vows of austerity."

Among the prostitutes, one attractive young girl spoke up: "I shall seduce Haridāsa within three days", she promised.

Rāmacandra Khān said to her, "My constable will go with you so that as soon as he sees you with Haridāsa, he will at once arrest him and bring both of you to me."

The prostitute replied, "First let me have union with him once; then the second time I shall take your constable with me to arrest him."

At night the prostitute dressed herself most attractively and went to the cottage of Haridāsa Ṭhākura with great jubilation. After offering obeisances to the tulasī plant, she went to Haridāsa's door, offered him obeisances and stood there. Exposing part of her body to his view, she sat down on the threshold and spoke to him in very sweet words.

"My dear Ṭhākura, O great preacher, great devotee, you are so beautifully built and your youth is just beginning. What woman could control her mind after seeing you? I'm eager to be united with you. My mind is greedy for this. If I don't obtain you, I won't be able to keep my body and soul together."

Haridāsa Ṭhākura replied, "I shall accept you without fail, but you will have to wait until I've finished chanting my regular rounds of the Hare Kṛṣṇa *mantra* on my beads. Until then, please sit and listen to the chanting of the holy name. As soon as I'm finished, I'll fulfill your desire."

Hearing this, the prostitute remained sitting there while Haridāsa chanted on his beads until the light of morning appeared. When she saw that it was morning, she stood up and left.

Coming before Rāmacandra Khān, she said, "Last night Haridāsa promised to enjoy with me. Tonight I shall certainly have union with him."

That night the prostitute came again and Haridāsa Ṭhākura gave her many assurances. "Last night you were disappointed. Please excuse my offense. I shall certainly accept you. Please sit down and hear the chanting of the Hare Kṛṣṇa *mahā-mantra* until my regular chanting is finished. Then I will surely fulfill your desire."

After bowing down to the tulasī plant and Haridāsa Ṭhākura, the prostitute sat down at the door. Hearing Haridāsa chanting the Hare Kṛṣṇa *mantra,* she also chanted "Hare Kṛṣṇa, Hare Kṛṣṇa, Kṛṣṇa Kṛṣṇa, Hare Hare/Hare Rāma, Hare Rāma, Rāma Rāma, Hare Hare."

At sunrise, the prostitute became restless. Seeing this, Haridāsa Ṭhākura spoke to her as follows.

"I have vowed to chant ten million names this month. I thought that last night I would surely finish my chanting, but I couldn't. Tonight I will surely finish and my vow will be fulfilled. Then I can enjoy with you in full freedom."

The prostitute returned to Rāmacandra Khān and told him what had happened. That night she went earlier to Haridāsa, just before sunset. After bowing down with great respect to the tulasī plant and Haridāsa, she sat down on the threshold of the room. As she heard Haridāsa Ṭhākura's chanting of the holy name, she again chanted along with him.

"Today I shall surely finish my chanting", Haridāsa Ṭhākura assured her. "Then I shall satisfy all your desires."

Once again the night ended while Haridāsa Ṭhākura was chanting, but by now his association had purified the prostitute's mind. She fell at Haridāsa's lotus feet and confessed that Rāmacandra Khān had appointed her to pollute him. "Being a prostitute, I've committed unlimited sins. O my lord, please be merciful to me! Deliver my fallen soul."

Haridāsa Ṭhākura replied, "I know everything about Rāmacandra Khān's conspiracy against me. He is nothing but an ignorant fool. On the very day he planned his intrigue against me, I would have left this place at once, but because you came to me I stayed here for three days to deliver you."

The prostitute said, "My dear *guru,* please tell me how I can get relief from material existence."

Haridāsa Ṭhākura replied, "Without delay go home and distribute to the *brāhmaṇas* whatever you have. Then return to this cottage and stay here forever in Kṛṣṇa consciousness. Chant the Hare Kṛṣṇa *mantra* continuously and render service to the tulasī plant by watering her and praying to her. In this way you will very soon achieve shelter at Kṛṣṇa's lotus feet."

With that, Haridāsa Ṭhākura stood up and left, continuously chanting Hare Kṛṣṇa, Hare Kṛṣṇa, Kṛṣṇa Kṛṣṇa, Hare Hare/Hare Rāma, Hare Rāma, Rāma Rāma, Hare Hare.

On Haridāsa Ṭhākura's order, the prostitute distributed to the *brāhmaṇas* whatever she had. As a sign of renunciation she shaved her head clean and donned a plain white sari and then she took up residence in the cottage. Following the practice of her spiritual master, she began chanting the holy name of Kṛṣṇa 300,000 times a day. She chanted throughout the entire day and night.

She worshiped the tulasī plant and instead of eating regularly she ate whatever food she received as alms. If nothing was supplied, she would fast. Thus by eating frugally and fasting she conquered her senses and as soon as her senses were controlled, symptoms of love of Godhead appeared in her person.

Thus the prostitute became a celebrated devotee. She became very advanced in spiritual life and many stalwart Vaiṣṇavas would come to visit her. Seeing the sublime character of the prostitute, they were astonished. They glorified the influence of Haridāsa Ṭhākura and offered him obeisances.

Lessons from the pastime of Haridāsa Ṭhākura and the prostitute:

1. The chanting of the holy name of Kṛṣṇa is such a powerful meditation that it can protect one from even the strongest allurements of the material world.

2. Association with great devotees of the Lord can purify even the most sinful and inspire them to give up their sin and take up devotional service.

3. We should take up a vow to chant a minimum number of names every day. Haridāsa Ṭhākura chanted 300,000. Śrīla Prabhupāda instructed that devotees in the International Society for Krishna Consciousness must chant a minimum of 27,648 names daily, equivalent to sixteen rounds of the Hare Kṛṣṇa *mantra* on a string of 108 japa beads. Please see page 76 for more instructions on chanting japa.

One form of meditation that devotees of Kṛṣṇa practice is meditation on service to Him. The following account is adapted from a section of Śrīla Prabhupāda's Nectar of Devotion called "Meditation". This book is a translation of the Sanskrit devotional classic Sri Bhakti-rasāmṛta-sindhu, a complete manual on bhakti-yoga. The original story comes from the Brahma-vaivarta Purāṇa, an ancient Sanskrit scripture describing the science of devotional service to Kṛṣṇa.

In the city of Pratiṣṭhānapura in South India lived a poor but righteous *brāhmaṇa* who was fully satisfied by virtue of his self-realization and God realization. He did not bear any ill will toward the Lord because of his poverty, for he thought that it must have resulted from some misdeeds he'd performed in a previous life and that Lord Kṛṣṇa was mercifully minimizing his suffering. Thus he lived very peacefully, his only sadness being that his poverty meant he could perform only simple services for the Lord.

Sometimes he went to hear great realized souls speak on Kṛṣṇa consciousness. At one such meeting he heard that someone who cannot physically perform devotional activities can do so by meditation and achieve the same benefit. The *brāhmaṇa* was overjoyed to learn that he could simply meditate on performing grand, elaborate devotional services for the Lord and He would accept them.

The very next morning the *brāhmaṇa* began his mental service (*manasa-seva*). After bathing in the holy river Godāvarī, he sat down in a secluded place on the riverbank and performed the breath-control exercises called *prāṇāyāma* to concentrate his mind. As soon as he had fixed his mind on the form of Lord Nārāyaṇa (a four-handed form of God), he began to visualize dressing the Lord very carefully in costly silken garments and adorning His body with splendid jeweled ornaments, a crown and other items. Then he respectfully bowed down before the Lord and began to visualize cleaning the temple very thoroughly. In his mind's eye he then filled hundreds of elaborately wrought gold and silver pots with holy water from the Godāvarī, the Ganges, the Yamunā and other sacred rivers. Next he collected all kinds of items for worship, including fresh fragrant flowers, ripe fruits of all variety and the finest incense and sandalwood pulp. All these items the *brāhmaṇa* placed before the Deity for His satisfaction. Then he performed the ceremony called *arati,* in which one formally offers the Lord sacred articles like incense, lamps and flowers and finally he completed his worship according to the principles given in the scripture.

For many years the *brāhmaṇa* followed this routine every day. Then one day in his meditation he visualized cooking some sweet rice-pudding for the Deity. But he was troubled because this kind of rice pudding was meant to be served cold and he was worried that it hadn't cooled down enough. So he touched the pot to find out if it was ready to offer the Lord. But the pot was so hot that he burned his finger and his meditation broke. Amazingly, though it was only in his meditation that he'd burned his finger, a blister was quickly forming — his finger was actually burned!

As the *brāhmaṇa* looked at his finger with puzzled astonishment, Lord Nārāyaṇa in Vaikuṇṭha, with the goddess of fortune Lakṣmī Devi seated beside Him, began to smile. Lakṣmī and her lady friends asked the Lord why He was smiling, but He wouldn't tell. Instead, He dispatched a spiritual airplane to bring the *brāhmaṇa* to the kingdom of God. When the *brāhmaṇa* stood in the presence of the Lord and His companions, the Lord explained the whole story. The fortunate *brāhmaṇa* then received an eternal place among the Lord's loving associates in Vaikuṇṭha, "the place beyond all pain".

Lessons from the story of the meditating brāhmaṇa:

1. The Lord is simultaneously in His abode and in the hearts of all. So He is aware of all our innermost thoughts. If we absorb ourselves in thoughts of service

to Him, He knows that and will accept our service even if we cannot perform it externally.

2. In any circumstance we should be satisfied with our material assets and should try to serve the Lord as best we can. Following His principle, in the end we will become fully purified and return home, back to Godhead.

Chapter Four

Meditation Means

(Excerpts from the teachings of His Divine Grace A.C. Bhaktivedanta Swami Prabhupāda)

Meditation means remembering, *smaraṇam.* There are nine different kinds of devotional service, of which *smaraṇam* is one process; the *yogī* remembers the form of Viṣṇu within his heart. Thus there were many devotees engaged in meditation on Lord Viṣṇu under the big banyan tree.

Śrīmad-Bhāgavatam (4.6.33)

The word *abhidhyāyet,* which is used in this verse, indicates that unless one's mind is fixed, one cannot meditate. The conclusion, therefore, is that *Meditation means* thinking of the Lord within. Whether one comes to that stage by the *aṣṭāṅga-yoga* system or by the method recommended in the *śāstras* especially for this present age — to constantly chant the holy name of the Lord — the goal is to meditate on the Supreme Personality of Godhead.

Śrīmad-Bhāgavatam (4.8.44)

Meditation means stopping all nonsensical activities, at least for the time being. Devotional service, however, not only puts an end to all nonsensical mundane activities, but also engages one in meaningful devotional activities.

Nectar of Instruction: verse 3

Meditation means concentration upon the lotus feet of the Lord. Lotus feet indicate the Supreme Personality of Godhead. But those who are impersonalists do not recognize the lotus feet of the Lord and therefore their object of meditation is something impersonal. The demigods express their mature verdict that persons who are interested in meditating on something void or impersonal cannot cross over the ocean of nescience. Such persons are simply imagining that they have become liberated. "O lotus-eyed Lord! Their intelligence is contaminated because they fail to meditate upon the lotus feet of Your Lordship. As a result of this neglectful activity, the impersonalists fall down again into the material way of conditioned life, although they may temporarily rise to the point of impersonal realization."

Krishna Book 2 : Prayers by the Demigods for Lord Kṛṣṇa in the Womb

Samādhi or *meditation, means* that one has to find the Supersoul within himself. One who is not free from sinful reactions cannot see the Supersoul. If a person has a jeweled locket in his necklace but forgets the jewel, it is almost as though he does not possess it. Similarly, if an individual soul meditates but does not actually perceive the presence of the Supersoul within himself, his meditation is useless."

Krishna Book 87: Prayers by the Personified Vedas

Those who think of something impersonal are not *yogīs.* Their meditation simply involves undergoing more and more labor (*kleśo 'dhikataras teṣām avyaktāsakta-cetasām* [*Bg.* 12.5]) and they cannot reach anything substantial. Therefore after meditation they say, "Come on, give me a cigarette. Come on, my throat is now dry. Give me a cigarette." That is not meditation. *Meditation means* thinking of Kṛṣṇa always (*satataṁ cintayanto mām* [*Bg.* 9.14]) and endeavoring to advance in Kṛṣṇa consciousness with a firm vow (*yatantaś ca dṛḍha-vratāḥ*).

Teachings of Queen Kunti 5: The Vision of Lotuses

Mr. Faill: Do you think transcendental meditation is helping people?

Śrīla Prabhupāda: They do not know what real meditation is. Their meditation is simply a farce—another cheating process by the so-called *svāmīs* and *yogīs.* You're asking me if meditation is helping people, but do you know what meditation is?

Mr. Faill: A stilling of the mind—trying to sit in the center without swinging either way.

Śrīla Prabhupāda: And what is the center?

Mr. Faill: I don't know.

Śrīla Prabhupāda: So everyone is talking very much about meditation, but no one knows what meditation actually is. These bluffers use the word "meditation", but they do not know the proper subject for meditation. They're simply talking bogus propaganda.

Mr. Faill: Isn't meditation valuable just to get people thinking right?

Śrīla Prabhupāda: No. *Real Meditation means* to achieve a state in which the mind is saturated with God consciousness. But if you do not know what God is, how can you meditate? Besides, in this age people's minds are so agitated that they cannot concentrate. I have seen this so-called meditation; they are simply sleeping and snoring. Unfortunately, in the name of God consciousness or "self-realization", many bluffers are presenting nonstandard methods of meditation without referring to the authorized books of Vedic knowledge. They are simply practicing another type of exploitation.

Science of Self Realization 5e: Meditation and the Self within

So meditation is a process for cleansing the heart. *Meditation means* to try to understand one's relationship with the Supreme.

Science of Self Realization 8a: Knowing the Purpose of Life

Meditation is also a recommended process. One should question, "What am I?" Just consider: Am I this body? No. Am I this finger? No, this is my finger. If you contemplate your leg, you will see, "Oh, this is my leg." Similarly, you will find everything to be "mine". And where is that "I"? Everything is mine, but where is that "I"? When one is searching for that "I", that is meditation. *Real Meditation means* concentrating all the senses in that way. But that meditation process is very difficult. One must control the senses. The senses are dragging one outward and one has to bring them inward for introspection. Therefore there are eight processes in the *yoga* system. The first is controlling the senses by regulative principles. Then sitting postures — that will help to concentrate the mind. If one sits leaning over, that will not help; if one sits up straight, that will help. Then controlling the breathing, then meditation, then *samādhi.*

Science of Self Realization 8a: Knowing the Purpose of Life

Meditation is thinking, but no one thinks of Kṛṣṇa; they think of void or something impersonal. If someone is thinking of Kṛṣṇa or Nārāyaṇa or Viṣṇu, as prescribed in the Vedic scriptures, that is real *yoga; yoga Meditation means* to focus one's mind upon the Supersoul. The Supersoul is the representation of Kṛṣṇa in the form of four-handed Nārāyaṇa. Even Patañjali, an authority on the yoga system, prescribes meditation on Viṣṇu. But just as people are manufacturing bogus religious processes, the so-called *yogīs* of today have manufactured their own way of thinking of something void.

Science of Self Realization 8b: The Highest Love

The entire *Bhagavad-gītā* is an inspiration to work, to engage in Kṛṣṇa consciousness, to act on Kṛṣṇa's behalf. Kṛṣṇa never tells Arjuna, "My dear friend Arjuna, don't concern yourself with this war. Just sit down and meditate upon Me." This is not the message of *Bhagavad-gītā.* We are not to refrain from all activity, but only from those activities that impede our consciousness of Kṛṣṇa. *Meditation means* stopping all nonsensical activity.

Those who are advanced in Kṛṣṇa consciousness are constantly working for Kṛṣṇa.

Path of Perfection 1: Yoga as Action

Bhakti means acting spiritually in accordance with the desires of Hṛṣīkeśa. How can we act? Since we must act with our senses, we must spiritualize our senses in order to act properly. As stated before, sitting in silent *Meditation means* stopping undesirable activity, but acting in Kṛṣṇa consciousness is transcendental. The cessation of nonsensical action is not in itself perfection. We must act perfectly. Unless we train our senses to act in accordance with Hṛṣīkeśa, the master of the senses, our senses will again engage in undesirable activities and we will fall down. Therefore we must engage the senses in action for Kṛṣṇa and in this way remain firmly fixed in Kṛṣṇa consciousness.

Path of Perfection 2: Mastering the Mind and Senses

Disciple: Socrates took the oracular *gnothi seauton,* "know thyself", to enjoin "care of the soul". Care of the soul, as we have seen, involved an intense intellectual endeavor, a kind of introspective contemplation or meditation. It gradually purified the self, detaching it more and more from the body and its passions. Thus through the contemplative endeavor entailed by "know thyself", a person attained knowledge and self-control and with that he also became happy.

Śrīla Prabhupāda: Yes, that is a fact. *Meditation means* analyzing the self and searching for the Absolute

Truth. That is described in the Vedic literatures: *dhyānāvasthita-tad-gatena manasā paśyanti yaṁ yoginaḥ* [*Śrīmad-Bhāgavatam* 12.13.1]. Through meditation, the *yogī* sees the Supreme Truth (Kṛṣṇa or God) within himself. Kṛṣṇa is there. The *yogī* consults with Kṛṣṇa and Kṛṣṇa advises him. That is the relationship Kṛṣṇa has with the *yogī*.

The Quest for Enlightenment 6b: Socrates: He Knew Himself — to a Certain Extent

So the *yogīs*, they are trying to come to this point by meditation, "Whether I am this body or not." *Meditation means* that. First meditation, concentration of the mind, the different kinds of sitting posture, that helps me to concentrate my mind. And if I concentrate my mind, meditation, so am I this body? Then if I am not this body, where I am in this body? Then if he analyzes, he'll find himself within this heart. Within this heart the soul is also there and the Supersoul is also there. Kṛṣṇa is also there. So the perfectional stage of yoga is to see the Supersoul and understand oneself that "I am individual soul". So that perfectional stages we are immediately offering, that you try to see Kṛṣṇa always, Kṛṣṇa consciousness. The *yogīs* are trying to reach a platform after so much exercise of the body. We are giving that thing immediately, that "Be Kṛṣṇa conscious". You are eternal part and parcel of Kṛṣṇa and Kṛṣṇa is the Supersoul. Why should you take so much botheration to find Him within? He's without also. He's all-powerful. He can accept your offerings and you can take *prasādam*.

This is practical yoga. So we are not beginning from the gross stage.

Bhagavad-gītā 2.13-17 — Los Angeles, November 29, 1968

Meditation means as you see the form of Kṛṣṇa and whenever you go, the impression of the form will be within your eyes and if you think of Kṛṣṇa, your life is successful. Therefore the Deity of Kṛṣṇa should be seen. That is the benefit of the eyes. The ears should be engaged hearing about Kṛṣṇa. The tongue should be engaged for eating Kṛṣṇa's remnants of foodstuff, *prasādam.* The nose should be engaged for smelling the flower which is offered to Kṛṣṇa or the *tulasī.* In this way, when you engage all your senses, the legs should be utilized for coming to this temple to see Kṛṣṇa. Not to going to the cinema rascal. Then your life will be successful. You'll understand Kṛṣṇa. Kṛṣṇa is very kind. He says *teṣāṁ satata-yuktānām* [*Bg.* 10.10], if you engage all your senses for understanding Kṛṣṇa with devotion and faith, *prīti-purvakam,* with love, the love is the basic principle of understanding Kṛṣṇa.

Bhagavad-gītā 4.9 — Bombay, March 29, 1974

Meditation is meant for the *satya-yuga.* What is that verse? *Kṛte yad dhyāyato viṣṇum* [*Śrīmad-Bhāgavatam* 12.3.52]. *Kṛte, kṛte* means *satya-yuga.* People were very restrained, all *paramahaṁsas.* In those days it was possible to meditate. At the present moment our mind is so disturbed, we are disturbed in so many ways.

Meditation is not possible in this age. Maybe there may be one or two persons who can meditate. The *Real Meditation means* to think of Kṛṣṇa. *Man-manā bhava mad-bhakto mad-yājī māṁ namaskuru* [*Bg.* 18.65]. That is real meditation.

Bhagavad-gītā 4.9 — Bombay, March 29, 1974

This *sāṅkhya-yoga* was first practiced by Kapiladeva. He is incarnation of God, Kṛṣṇa. So this is the secret of *yoga.* That this, I mean to say, process of sitting and seeing the tip of your nose and sitting straight, all these means will help you to concentrate your mind on the Viṣṇu form or Kṛṣṇa. One should meditate upon Me. This *Meditation means* meditation on Kṛṣṇa. So here in this Kṛṣṇa consciousness movement, it is directly simply on Kṛṣṇa. There is nothing, therefore nobody is better meditator than these boys. They are simply concentrating on Kṛṣṇa. Their whole business is Kṛṣṇa. They're working in the garden, digging the earth, "Oh, there will be nice rose, we shall offer to Kṛṣṇa." Meditation. Practical meditation. I shall grow rose and it will be offered to Kṛṣṇa. Even in the digging there is meditation. You see? They are preparing nice foodstuff, "Oh, it will be eaten by Kṛṣṇa." So in cooking there is meditation. You see? You see? And what to speak of chanting and dancing. So they are meditating twenty-four hours in Kṛṣṇa. Perfect *yogī.* Let anyone come and challenge. These boys are perfect *yogīs.*

Bhagavad-gītā 6.13-15 — Los Angeles, February 16, 1969

Prabhupāda: That means these are manufacturing. Actually, there is no fixed-up knowledge. Just like somebody was asking (about) transcendental meditation. What is that transcendental meditation? Can anyone explain?

Devotee: I went to one of their meetings and it was just..., they talk about something concentrating, feeling, something going down, like, something coming up. But it's just...

Prabhupāda: Not very, I mean to say, clear. Something vague. So this will not help. Here is positive proposition, that you concentrate on the form of Kṛṣṇa. *Mayy āsakta-manāḥ pārtha. Yoginām api sarveṣāṁ mad-gatenāntar-ātmanā śraddhāvān... Antar-ātmanā* [*Bg.* 6.47]. One has to fix up the form... Actual *yoga* system is to concentrate on the form of Viṣṇu. *Dhyānāvasthita-tad-gatena manasā.* By... *Meditation means* to concentrate the mind without being diverted to any other subject. Simply thinking of Lord Viṣṇu. That is the *yoga* meditation recommended in Vedic literature. So here also, Kṛṣṇa says "Me". Kṛṣṇa and Viṣṇu, the same. Viṣṇu is expansion of Kṛṣṇa. So when we concentrate our mind upon Kṛṣṇa, Viṣṇu is included there.

Bhagavad-gītā 7.1 — San Diego, July 1, 1972

Meditation means to fix up one's mind on the Supreme Personality of Godhead. First of all they do not know who is the Personality of Godhead. But the *yoga* practice, according to *śāstra,* is that. Here it is: *mayy āsakta-manāḥ pārtha yogam.* This is *yoga.* In other

Vedic literature that is also stated, the same thing. *Dhyānāvasthita-tad-gatena manasā paśyanti yaṁ yoginaḥ* [*Śrīmad-Bhāgavatam* 12.13.1]. *Yogī* means who meditates. It is the business of the *yogīs* to meditate. But if you do not know upon whom to meditate, then what is the meaning of your *yoga?* Therefore I have seen practically in America. There are so many *yoga* societies. They close their eyes and I do not know what they are meditating, but I have seen, they are snoring. (laughter) And what they will do? (makes snoring sound) (laughter) This is *yoga* system. So don't be misled by these bluffers' *yoga* system. Don't be misled. Here is *yoga,* Kṛṣṇa, because *yoga* means to meditate upon the Supreme, *dhyānāvasthita-tad-gatena manasā,* mind fully absorbed and they see Kṛṣṇa or Nārāyaṇa, the same thing.

Bhagavad-gītā 7.1 — London, March 9, 1975

Very simple. *Īśvaraḥ,* that God, in His Paramātmā feature is sitting within everyone's heart, your heart, my heart, everyone's. God is... You haven't got to find out God somewhere else. Therefore the *yogīs,* they practice, "How to find out God within myself?" That is called meditation. *Meditation means* to find out... It is heard from the *śāstra,* "The God is within my heart. Now let me find out where is God within my heart." That is called *yoga, yoga* system. *Dhyānāvasthita-tad-gatena manasā paśyanti yaṁ yoginaḥ* [*Śrīmad-Bhāgavatam* 12.13.1]. *yogī's* business is to become engaged in meditation, *dhyānāvasthita.* Now this meditation is very profusely used in your country especially. But what is the meditation? This is meditation. When you fix up your mind to find out God, Kṛṣṇa, within your heart, that is called meditation, not thinking some foolish objective is meditation. This is meditation. *Dhyānāvasthita-tad-gatena manasā. Tad-gatena,* mind being fully absorbed in Him, by that mind, you can find out.

Bhagavad-gītā 16.6 — Hawaii, February 2, 1975

So purification means getting free gradually from sex desire and this is attained by *meditation* on the person of the Lord as described herein, beginning from the feet. One should not try to go upwards artificially without seeing for himself how much he has been released from the sex desire.

Śrīmad-Bhāgavatam (2.2.12)

Chapter Five

Meditation in Kṛṣṇa Consciousness

Members of the Kṛṣṇa consciousness movement practice several types of meditation in order to elevate consciousness from the material level to the transcendental level. We shall now review them.

Meditation on the Self as Different from the Body

The first step in meditation is to understand that the self is not the body. If we meditate carefully we can see that the body is like a vehicle for the conscious self. We can meditate on the hand and we can understand that the hand is not the real self. We can observe it, we can will that it move. We can understand that it is "my hand". But who is the "I" that possesses the hand and who calls the hand "mine"? That is the real self. If we analyze every other part and limb of the body, we come to the same conclusion. The parts of the body or even all of the parts together, are not the self. The self is something different. The self is different even than the mind. The mind is full of thoughts, but we are not those thoughts. We are the self that is conscious of the thoughts. In the *Bhagavad-gītā* (13.4), Lord Kṛṣṇa says, "O son of Bharata, as the sun alone illuminates all this universe, so does the living entity, one within the body, illuminate the entire body by consciousness." We can also see that the body is changing, but the conscious self remains the same. We can therefore conclude that the self will survive the end of the current body. The *Gītā* (2.13) says, "As the embodied soul continuously passes, in this body, from boyhood to youth to old age, the soul similarly passes into another body at death. A sober person is not bewildered by such a change."

Meditation on the Supersoul

By careful meditation we can perceive the presence of the Supersoul. We have already seen that the self is different than the body. But we can also observe by careful meditation how the conscious soul takes help from the intelligence. The intelligence gives us direction. For example, if we are standing on a busy street and wish to cross, then we have to take the help of our intelligence. If the intelligence is functioning properly, then we look carefully both ways and if it is safe to cross, the intelligence will tell us to cross. But what is the source of this intelligence, which we are consulting hundreds of times a day? The intelligence is coming to us from the Supersoul. According to our degree of surrender to the Supersoul, we will get a certain kind of material or spiritual intelligence, which will direct us in a certain way. Those who are very much influenced by the mode of ignorance will get intelligence that directs them in a way that outside observers will recognize as deranged.

Those who are very much influenced by the mode of passion, will get an intelligence that allows them to act very successfully in the realm of material acquisition and influence. And those whose intelligence is influenced by the mode of goodness, will be directed toward spiritual life. When one is very much absorbed in the activities of spiritual progress, God Himself gives good intelligence. As Kṛṣṇa says in the *Bhagavad-gītā* (10.10), "To those who are constantly devoted to serving Me with love, I give the understanding by which they can come to Me".

Meditation on the Form of God

At the present moment, our material senses are not able to directly perceive the spiritual form of God. But God, being merciful, makes Himself available in a form that we can see. The form may be of paint or wood or stone or metal. But if the form of God is represented authentically in these materials, then God can agree to become present in this form and it can be meditated upon successfully. According to meditation techniques described in the *Śrīmad-Bhāgavatam* and other writings, the meditation should begin at the feet and continue upwards until one reaches the smiling face of the Lord. The *Śrīmad-Bhāgavatam* (2.2.13) says, "The process of meditation should begin from the lotus feet of the Lord and progress to His smiling face. The meditation should be concentrated upon the lotus feet, then the calves, then the thighs and in this way higher and higher. The more the mind becomes fixed upon the different parts of the limbs, one after another, the more the intelligence becomes purified."

Meditation on God in Nature

A spiritual meditator learns to see the presence of God in everything, including the wonders of nature. In the *Bhagavad-gītā,* Lord Kṛṣṇa says: "I am the taste of water, the light of the sun and the moon" (7.8); "I am the original fragrance of the earth and I am the heat in fire" (7.9); "of bodies of water I am the ocean" (10.24); "of immovable things I am the Himalayas" (10.25); "of all trees I am the banyan tree" (10.26); "among beasts I am the lion" (10.30); "of fishes I am the shark and of flowing rivers I am the Ganges" (10.31); "of seasons I am flower-bearing spring" (10.35); and "I am victory, I am adventure and I am the strength of the strong" (10.36).

Meditation on the Pastimes of God

People meditate quite a bit on the activities of famous people. People want to know about their favorite personalities: With whom are they romantically involved? Where are they going? What are they doing? What is their history? There is a huge media industry dedicated to providing the public with the material for such meditation. But in the end, there is little benefit from such meditation. As for the stars themselves, they remain caught in the cycle of birth and death, suffering the miseries of old age and disease, as well as legal difficulties. And their fans also remain caught in the same cycle, simply getting a little relief from their own problems by meditating upon those of the more famous objects of their attention. But meditating upon the pastimes of Lord Kṛṣṇa is different. When He appears on earth, Lord Kṛṣṇa displays amazing transcendental pastimes, recorded in the pages of literatures such as *Śrīmad-Bhāgavatam.* These pastimes are called *nitya-lila,* eternal pastimes. Kṛṣṇa is beyond birth and death and by meditating on His eternal pastimes, we become qualified to enter into them ourselves. And then we also become beyond birth and death. Lord Kṛṣṇa says in the *Bhagavad-gītā* (4.9), "One who knows the transcendental nature of My appearance and activities does not, upon leaving the body, take his birth again in this material world, but attains My eternal abode, O Arjuna."

Very advanced devotees meditate upon the most confidential pastimes of Lord Kṛṣṇa, His pastimes with the *gopis,* the cowherd girls of Vrindavan. These eternal associates of the Lord express their love for Him in a way that resembles the dealings of boys and girls in the material world. Actually, the dealings of boys and girls in the material world are a distorted reflection of the pastimes of Kṛṣṇa and the *gopis* in the spiritual world. In the spiritual world there is no sex as we understand it in the bodily conception of life, but there is a spiritual exchange of emotions that resembles the exchange of emotions between boys and girls in this world. Descriptions of the dealings between Kṛṣṇa and the *gopis* can be found in the 10th Canto of the *Śrīmad-Bhāgavatam.* These pastimes cannot be properly understood by those who are under the influence of material sex desire. Nevertheless, if one hears about them from the proper sources and controls the desire for material sex relations, one can experience pure transcendental pleasure.

Meditation on Service to God

We all have our original spiritual personalities, but in our present state in the material world it is as if we are suffering from amnesia and paralysis. We have forgotten Kṛṣṇa and our identities as Kṛṣṇa's eternal servants. And we have lost our ability to use our senses in Kṛṣṇa's service. Some of the more passive kinds of transcendental meditation help us reawaken our awareness of our original spiritual identity, but there is also a kind of active meditation that helps us gradually become able to regain the control and actions of our spiritual senses. Our spiritual senses are now covered by matter. These senses are of two kinds: (1) knowledge acquiring senses like the eyes, ears, nose, tongue and skin and (2) working senses, like the arms, legs, voice and genitals. These covered senses are now being employed in selfish material activities that keep us in the cycle of birth and death. It is as if the spiritual senses are paralyzed. In some cases a paralyzed person can regain the functions of his limbs by engaging in physical therapy under the guidance of experts. So in the same way, we can regain the functions of our now dormant spiritual senses by engaging in spiritual therapy under the guidance of spiritual experts who can teach us gradually, step by step, how to use our present senses in such a way that we get back the functions of our spiritual senses, which are part of a spiritual body. In this way, we become prepared for entering the eternal life of service to Kṛṣṇa in the spiritual world. Just as astronauts receive special training before entering the new environment of space, we also need training before we can enter the new environment of the spiritual world. Part of this training is learning how to meditate on Kṛṣṇa while performing actions for the satisfaction of Kṛṣṇa. When this art is mastered, action itself becomes a kind of meditation.

Japa Mantra Meditation

Japa is the chanting of a *mantra* in a low voice usually using a string of beads for counting. The chanting of the Hare Kṛṣṇa *mantra* in the form of japa meditation is one of the foundational spiritual practice of the Kṛṣṇa consciousness movement. Japa meditation is performed on a strand of 108 wooden beads (see "A Beginner's Guide to Kṛṣṇa Consciousness", pg. 33). The beads are made from the wood of the *tulasī* tree, a tree sacred to Kṛṣṇa. The number 108 represents the 108 principal associates of Kṛṣṇa, the *gopis.* Although the Hare Kṛṣṇa *mantra* can be chanted by anyone, to get the maximum effect from the *mantra,* one should receive it from a spiritual master in the line of disciplic succession coming from Kṛṣṇa Himself. At the time of initiation one vows to chant the Hare Kṛṣṇa *mantra* a certain number of times a day, as determined by the *guru.* In the International Society for Kṛṣṇa Consciousness, initiated members vow to chant sixteen rounds on their beads. In other words, they chant the *mantra* 108 × 16 times a day (1,728 times). Initiates also vow to follow four regulative principles: (1) no eating meat, fish or eggs; (2) no illicit sex; (3) no intoxication; (4) no gambling. By following these principles, meditators are able to remove obstacles that block one from receiving the full benefit of chanting the Hare Kṛṣṇa *mantra.*

Silent Mantra Meditation

In order to help the meditator get even more effect from the Hare Kṛṣṇa *mantra,* the meditator can after a couple of years take a second initiation into the chanting of the gayatri *mantras.* This set of *mantras* is chanted silently at the three junctures of the day, sunrise, noon and sunset. From time immemorial the gayatri *mantras* have been chanted by the *brāhmaṇas* in India.

Congregational Meditation

As contradictory as it seems, the most powerful form of meditation is kirtan or group meditation. We see some reflection of this spiritual reality in material events. For example, when at a football game, the supporters of the "home" team become united in cheering for a victory. This, however, is just a reflection of the powerful effects of people joining together to chant the Hare Kṛṣṇa *mantra.* It is like entering into a churning ocean of spiritual energies. The benefits can be realized not only by those participating in the actual chanting, but by those who simply witness it. This congregational chanting was especially recommended by Lord Caitanya, who appeared in West Bengal about five hundred years ago. Lord Caitanya was an incarnation of God who appeared to teach the meditation system for this present age. He especially recommended the congregational chanting of the holy names of God. Any genuine name of God will work — Kṛṣṇa, Rāma, Allah, Jehovah, according to one's taste.

The Goal

The goal is to practice all these kinds of meditation in combination so that the mind is focused on Kṛṣṇa all the time. This unbroken state of meditation is called *samādhi* or trance. In this state, one is freed from fear and anxiety. One is freed from unnecessary attachment to material things. This does not mean that one has no material possessions. Rather it means that one sees whatever possessions one has as the energy of God, to be employed in God's service. So whether one is living with very few possessions or one is living with great opulence, one remains absorbed in *samādhi* and whatever one has, one uses for the service of God and God's creatures. In this state, one experiences inner peace, satisfaction and pleasure and maintains friendly relations with all living things. At the end of life, one is qualified to enter the spiritual world, to join the eternal spiritual pastimes of Lord Kṛṣṇa.